DECLINE
of the
ANIMAL
KINGDOM

DECLINE
of the
ANIMAL
KINGDOM

LAURA CLARKE

poems

ECW Press | a mîsFît book

To my family

Contents

I.

Vigour

What is sometimes characterized as stubbornness is simply the
mule's ability to think for itself and make decisions for its own
protection and the safety of its rider.
— CANADIAN DONKEY & MULE ASSOCIATION

Nine-tenths hybrid vigour, one-tenth reproductive
tragedy, bound by moonlit manure, the overlap
of hoof and paw in fresh mud, feathers pushed
through shining millimetres of chicken wire.

The gulf between the 62nd and 64th chromosome
spans dusty gum on fence posts, drifts on currents
of browned river scum, rests within the red pinpoint
in the horsefly's eye when it chooses you.

Find a Molly or John to birth you viable offspring?
That's like, you know. Needle in a haystack, haystack
in the palm of a hand, a velvet ear in a hand, hands
all over you, disappointed hands on a slippery birth.

And if you were hoping your blink would attract
the red of a thousand flies if you were still enough,
if you were workhorse enough, as if science
would melt in the hick sun like neon crayons

flung in an incubator, as if affinity for the plough
counted in the long run, as if you could be a bad omen
to Herodotus and not be changed. Well.
You should know better, sweet thing.

Attention! All Ye Beasts of Miraculous Origins

The males tried to stomp you to death,
catch your shaky newborn legs underfoot
and break them, and the females tried
to take you for their own,
offering up centuries-dormant nipples
and sure-footed love.

Cum mula peperit: the world ends
as it's sucked into the centre of a walnut
crushed in a spring storm last summer.
The foal greys and disintegrates in 24 hours
under a blue moon. Your name is contested
in a *Mules and More* contest.

History rides you hard, but you like it that way.
Your knees wobble but gain ground.
Aristotle hears a rumour of your birth
among tractor parts and razorblades,
wins the 2007 name game by a landslide.

Does hemiclonal transmission mean you belong to no one?

Baby, miracles only happen 50 times every 200 years.
You always were a fatherless beast,
pulsing with joke chromosomes —
amphibious, more toad than horse,
more frog than donkey. The flies knew
and liked to hover, just out of reach.

John Picks Up

If the length of the penis were a sign of honor, then the mule would belong to the Quraysh.
— AL-JAHIZ, BOOK OF THE MULES

We can do it all night.
No need to spend $9.99 on XL Durex
at the only Shoppers in town.

No need for a pregnancy test,
unless we're part of some larger miracle,
and we both know we're not.

I'm a foot and a half of pure virility, sorry,
sterility, bound only
by a fence edged in electricity.

Your mane stands on end
every time your hide brushes wire.
So let's make the most of it.

We both love the way abandoned saddles
look in the moonlight.
Let's stay out here a little longer.

I'll tell you about a foal I saw birthed.
The noise wrapping around tractors
and scratching DL + BZ 4 EVER

in barnyard wood.
The slick afterbirth in the grass,
shining in the sun.

Dead Mule Zone I: Falls From Cliffs

I've always made the decision to put one
in front of the other, lug like a silk-eared champion,

guide like a wise man with a grungy tail,
wake and sleep as a blurry, yellowing force,

so why stop now, when the red line
of cliff edge tells me to continue,

when the brush grows towards scruffy clouds
just like that, when clumps of dirt fall away

in mid-air as though they always belonged
to the bottom of the ravine? To stop

is to be anti-wind, to deny, to make a death
cap grow downwards, to walk backwards

and place the robin's egg gently in its nest.

Three-Domain System

· I ·

Shivering grey triangle of mouse,
toothpick leg floppy under steel wire
in a dusty trap on the hottest night in July,

what the fuck are you doing here?
You leave delicate shits on soup cans,
skitter across the ancient linoleum nightly,

jolting me awake, my body star-fished
in a spasm of primordial nerves bracing
for a long fall against white sheets.

When you die of heart failure in 10 minutes,
I'll scoop you up with a plastic bag
and place you gently in the garbage chute,

imagine a faint thump when you reach the end,
get sentimental, recite a prayer,
half of Psalm 23:4, what I remember of it.

I don't believe in God, but I pray often.
Like a couple of times a week.

· II ·

In a dusty cabinet, antique glass birds cluster:
nestled among them, small eggs,
impossibly blue like Easter chocolate,
symmetrical holes in thin shells

where he inserted a sewing needle
and gently blew the contents into a toilet bowl,
expelling a robin embryo
that was only a pinprick of blood nestled in yolk.

And that's how it goes, dear egg — just 'cause
you're fertilized, there's no guarantee.

Dead Mule Zone II:
Decapitation by Irate Opera Singer

Santa Fe County Police Report, July 15, 1956, 2:49 a.m.

Officer 1:

He couldn't stop doing the opposite of what she wanted,
compulsively, obsessively, heroically. Historically.
He tried hard to be the horse she always wanted,
to take the bit, embrace direction and affection,
rejoice at dry carrot, bite gently around the mould.

Officer 2:

She swore if you cut him open and lay out his entrails,
they would spell PERVERSE. Anti-contralto.
What else would compel him sing to his reflection
in a dull shiny knife, sing against his nature,
keep singing while the knife cut in?

Officer 1:

She did it because. Most things are unstoppable —
one red brick crumbles beneath another,
an ivory-carved pair of dice lands two sixes up,
a chalk heart encircles tomato seeds on the sidewalk.

Officer 2:

Questioning lasted eight hours and yielded
frustrating results. There is a hard limit
to everything. The length of a song;
the affection you give to a dog.

Architeuthis

When I finally saw the giant squid, I was like,
it's not that big. My dog pissed a heart shape
on the sidewalk and it was bigger than that.
I wanted the squid to go on forever, elephantine
subspherical suckers with finely serrated rings
of chitin, lively tentacles circling space and emerging
in the future, waving, eyes like soulful car tires,
ecstatic ink clouds enveloping birch trees and bridges.

Scientists brought the eye to my house
to demonstrate its close proximity in size
to a dinner platter, explaining only an extinct
aquatic reptilian predator matched the diameter
of its unblinking pupil, 9 centimetres or 3.5 inches.
Predictably, they placed it on an actual dinner platter,
and it looked right past me. In my own house.

Dear squid eye / dinner platter combo:
once my ex-boyfriend was hired to transport
plumbing supplies in Ottawa, becoming
so hopelessly lost in his oversized vehicle,
he was fired by end of day. The warehouse
was 20 minutes away, but he drove that truck
straight into the province of Quebec.

Messianic Age

CL > MISSED CONNECTIONS > TORONTO > w4d

I saw you at Edward and Chestnut, and earlier,
Queen and Bay, sitting demurely among man-made shrubs

and red pebbles, bravely enacting a solo nativity scene
nobody else could see. Maybe you were stressed out

by the symbolic burden of the whole event,
tired of standing for something besides you since 7 a.m.,

exhausted from evoking tender abstract feelings
in every person who glimpsed your wide ears,

that you tucked those dainty legs under your torso
and rested. Let yourself be hypnotized

by the dry cleaning sign rotating against a grey sky.
You should have headed north, past

the glowing promise of REAL LIVE NUDE
INTERACTIVE DANCING, past the dance music–

reverberating red pickup on Yonge, transporting
headless mannequins advertising two-for-one T-shirts,

plastic asses stuffed into acid-washed jeans,
neck stubs blooming into baseball caps.

To your credit, you went for it, heroically jumping
the POLICE DO NOT CROSS yellow tape,

enduring a tranquilizer dart in the hind leg, mimicking
the image of noble leaping deer on my travel mug.

You slept outside a Subway, feigned indifference
to fawning fans, chose breakneck getaway spectacle

over an afternoon nap. I like your style, deer.
I wish you would have hung around.

Dead Mule Zone III:
Rabies

Dog:

How do you make a mule fall for you?

Fold this 8.5 x 11 piece of paper into the shape
you think he thinks he deserves.

Serve it up on the palm of any hand,
in any circumstance or weather.

Mule:

A list of what we mistake for love:

scratching our backs on an upturned
stick in cold mud.

Running far from water, hydro-
phobia brewing, splitting our hairs.

Dog:

Acute inflammation of the brain
in warm-blooded animals.

Mythic mouth froth, delirium,
agitation. A casual midday
conversation gone zoonotic.

Mule:

To be held in jaws so white.
Even for a second.

Urkingdom

The cactus flower shifts a millimetre to the right,
learns to avoid the sunbeam, imperceptibly
and against its nature, registers the thrill of green
shrivelling to brown, registers the rub of dirt
against root, blooms in spite of itself.

You kneel before a 23-year-old who directs you
in a clear and confident Newfoundland accent
while yanking your hair, which tangles so infinitely
you cut several dreadlocked strands away in the morning,
discover a new freckle below your earlobe.

The moth's wings disintegrate on the windowsill,
silky powder a surprise for hands anticipating
coarseness of dust or flaked paint chips,
fingerprints brought to life in a smudge of white
against glass before being wiped away by a sleeve.

The park tree shades skateboarding French bulldogs
and frayed soccer nets, multi-coloured plastic straws
flashing colour in gravel. A branch taps the window
with a three-pronged twig. A man bent over
a cheap telescope jerks upwards to look at you.

Bear Safety Tips for Semi-Regular Trips to a Cabin in Algonquin Park

If you encounter a black bear,
it is likely to react in one of four ways.
— ALGONQUIN PROVINCIAL PARK NEWSLETTER

· I ·

Wake to paddles slapping water. Stage whispers scrape
pine trees, land on emerald ash borer–infested firewood,
squeeze through dusty screens.

Chipmunks rustle for attention in blueberry plants,
cast black bear shadows across the rusty barbeque.
Sunshine illuminates pork fat.

In most cases, a bear will hear or smell you before you are aware of it.

Especially if your dog has her period.
Especially if you drink a mickey of Fireball and spin
an antique globe, watching pastel colours blur
while you yell-explain the tragic nature of *Animorphs*.

· II ·

Yesterday, floating on my back, studying the sway
of yellow birch, I was almost run over by waving
German tourists in a fibreglass canoe.

Habituated bears: some lose their fear of humans from frequent contact.

Some people lose their desire to cook or wash their hair
or leave their house. From frequent contact. From habitat.

· III ·

I sit in the outhouse, cranking the windup flashlight.

Tacked into the rough wood are yellowing *Family Circus* cartoons,
spiderwebs shot across them. Fly carcasses dot the outer edges
of newspapers like punch lines.

Reacting to a defensive bear: do not climb a tree —
bears are excellent climbers.

Your best course of action is to stay in the outhouse forever.
The image of you growing old — crying over 20-year-old comics
until your fingers blacken with newsprint and the paper
dissolves into dust, which in turn clings to the spider's leg —
is kind of arousing.

· IV ·

A dock spider springs from the chalky rocks enclosing the fire,
dragging a filmy sac as large as her own quarter-sized body.

I'll feel those little spider children for weeks on my arms,
and how are any of us to know what the tickle
of near-invisible
silver limbs feels like at night alone?

Reacting to a fleeing black bear:
Enjoy the fleeting sight of a wild black bear.

Reacting to a fleeing anything:
Enjoy the fleeting sight of a _____.

Past & Future Lives with My Best Friend, Who Is Mushrooms

I held your pulsing gills in my right hand,
then I lost you. I wanted nobody to have you,
so I buried you under the dog house,

fed you blue jay bones and coffee grounds.
I sought you out. Described textures on internet
forums, scanned craigslist for seed catalogue romances.

Passed time by playing old-fashioned 20th century
games like pick-up sticks, hard-to-get, let's-get-fucked-up.
Chased the double halo on the 7-Eleven sign for decades,

embraced triple fecundation. Got real dirty.
Spent centuries waiting for you in laboratory
cow dung heaps, watching *Law & Order* reruns.

Paid good money to eat the last of your shrivelled
brown caps in a shining Amsterdam storefront,
dry mouth triumphant, only to have you spring

to abundance in a Texas Walmart parking lot.
Heard about your miraculous rebirth from an internet
know-it-all. Thought about burning the shopping plaza

to the ground but fire makes you stronger, stem yawning
and turning in dirt as forests and civilizations burn.
Buddy, please demonstrate how nourishment

is the most natural thing in the world. Show me how
patience can be fermented, teach me solitary confinement
and surprises. I'm the one left here as the hurricane

approaches, clutching bales of hay teeming with spores,
waiting for the eyewall to uplift you, redistribute you
behind a pile of tires in a meadow in Georgia.

Did You Know? Fun Facts About Mules

Mules are sterile and cannot reproduce. However they are anatomically normal and males must be gelded.

There was a boy who fed apples to the Shetland ponies just so he could wrap his hands around the electric fence. Kind of like when your cousin slit his wife's throat open and locked himself in the garage with the gas on.

Mules are a "made-to-order" breed of livestock. These fine animals can carry you safely on a trail, pack in the high country, compete in the show ring or pull logs and other equipment.

He didn't manage to kill either of them. And those fine black hairs will never fully come off your grandma's hand-knit shawl. Wet cloths don't work. Vacuums don't work. The preciseness of your hands doesn't work. Might as well weave them in.

Mules are popular for many reasons. Pleasure riders find that mules are smooth to ride, sure-footed and careful.

There was a woman. No, she wasn't pretty. Pretend I'm Nick Cave or a male poet or a female poet — there's nothing like a serial killer's eloquent voice and moonlight and the trunk of a car and a winding road. The sound of middle-aged neighbours arguing about terrariums will drive you crazy in a sunlit apartment on the third floor. Sorry, him crazy. In any season.

The mule combines the best features of both of its parents.

Do regurgitated greens strangle your appetite? Do you only eat when you're hungry? Do you abuse laxatives two to three times a week? Do you think the people and animals you murder in your dreams will haunt you, not figuratively haunt your thoughts, but haunt you like real ghosts?

From the donkey sire, the mule gets intelligence, ease of keeping, sure-footedness and longevity. The mare usually determines the size of the mule, its length of stride, style and conformation.

I killed my neighbour with a chainsaw in a dream. I didn't mean to. Still, I had to gather up the body parts in my own small hands and bury them, and that changed me, both in the dream and in real life.

I.

II.

Address to Husky and Fire Hydrant

Scruffy husky, tied to fire hydrant
With dollar store rhinestone collar,
Which way to the bingo hall?

I'm just a pair of legs
Marching past an army of slow walking teen moms,
In need of clear directions,

Just a flashing scowl
Glimpsed in the corner
Of a driver's eye at a red light.

Strands of hair pulled out
And left behind on a park bench
The moment the temperature hit +2.

Shoelaces neatly braided and looped
Around a pigeon's soft neck.

The 7-Elevens are closing down around me.

The laundromat closes at nine, not 10,
And the adult movie theatre's third neon X
Burnt out five days ago.

The bikers gathering on the same night
In the Tim Hortons parking lot for eight years
Is the sense of comfort
I've been seeking all along.

The women playing bingo past midnight
In the yellowing artificial light will never
Age, as long as they remain there,
Winning.

In Defence of My Buying Two Mules to Be Shot, Stuffed and Exhibited at the American Museum of Agriculture in Lubbock, Texas

Officer, we now know they were 10 and 12 years old respectively,
but I swear they told me they were 28.
If you hadn't been visited in your dreams by persistent beasts
asking for immortality by any means necessary,
you might think the whole situation unseemly.

To be euthanized for exhibit, to be put to work,
to be a key player in a tableau of agricultural revolutionaries
under a fake 19th century sun — to pull a McCormick reaper
for eternity with nothing but your patience and taxidermy-brown hide.
It's hard to ask for, even if it's what you want.

The *Daily News* attempted to contact the American Museum
of Agriculture, but did not receive a response. That's because
I'm locked in a staring contest with a delicate-horned slug
on my windowsill, and he's swishing his tail quite hypnotically.
Please email mules_28@hotmail.com for all other inquiries

about the nature of heroism, my views on human vs. animal
afterlife and practical tips for at-home taxidermy. Trust me,
you can see a lot with marble eyes. When the three of us ride off
into the fixed sunset, it never rains, and no fibreglass replica could
ever choose so swiftly between elevators and emergency exit,
could never reek of such hay-flecked instinct.

Materials for a Memoir
on Animal Locomotion

*There are two things in life I cannot do without: one is whiskey
and the other is Worcestershire sauce. Joy is neither.*
— GEORGE ADAMSON

It's natural to make to-do lists in the wild.
Friday: tighten muscles, drink eight glasses of water,
teach tautology to lions. Wednesday: stalk prey,

floss teeth, go into town for liquor.
Time, of course, is sun and mud and greasy tendons
no matter how many watches you stash in a tin cup.

Lists were made for the jungle, paper the proper
barometer for human behaviour in all elements —
super cute when dragged down by currents,

curls up submissively in extreme heat. Like you,
the leopard's lists are concerned with mating,
hunting, social activities. Rip off boy's left hand

between 1 and 4 p.m. on Thursday. Add to your list:
laundry, meditation, boiling water. Add to your list:
acquire mouthguard, hand paint lists and preserve

under glass. Boy. Girl. Boy. Girl. Gone wild.
Sunday: attack visiting family member or personal
assistant. Like you, the leopard wants it rougher

and rougher each time. Tuesday: escalate desire
to the point where completion becomes impossible.
Scan the list of things I can't live without: whiskey

and Worcestershire sauce. You are neither.
Add to that list weekend company, invisible ink.
Add to that list natural disasters, dust.

Born Free: A Lioness of Two Worlds

Find me down by the river babbling
lion-related puns to a lion:
you're the main event, baby.

Seeds look ugly as ever planted in a row.
All fur, all arguments, all the time.

The sun is always so orange on Tuesdays.
Instinct looks so strange written in crayon.

One time somewhere a lion jumped 36 feet
horizontally. You want to be awed.
I feel you.

Extinction

I grew my arm hair in a brick pattern
and smoked against my neighbour's wall.
Camouflage makes me soulful but reckless
e.g. eating cricket pie in plain daylight.
I foraged Tylenol 3s in the underbrush
from the old country, slept alone in fur pelts
under karaoke signs. Followed the moronic
koala's example and spearheaded evolutionary
stomach voodoo, got addicted to one food
that's really hard to find and grows scarcely
on mountaintops. The koala deserves to die,
like the Madagascar butterfly deserves
to be framed and hung above my toilet.
I really don't have the time to take care
of you anymore. You go be with your leopards,
and I'll be with my lions. It's a pride thing —
they can't coexist in close proximity so let's be
the kind of strangers who take each other
down in an open field while grazing.
If we were birds, I'd eat your young, chew
on a highlighter, and regurgitate fluorescent bones
in a patch of sunlight. But really, please send
updates on the progress of your pack
with clearly demarcated designations of *wild*
or *free*. Don't include yourself.
I'll be here in my tent. As always.

Carnivora

Grief in the summer is impossible,
so give me time. I'll hitchhike

into town with a plastic bucket,
get drunk at a dive bar, make a pact

with worms to live in dirt.
I'll speed-eat red meat. Refuse

first aid. Promise I'll grow forepaws
heavy enough to break a zebra's back.

Promise I'll return your library books.
It was all too hasty. Sitting here

with a canvas backpack, two stoned
tourists, and a trunk full of instant oatmeal.

Please send help. It's convenient, right?
You forget you live parallel to violence

just like me. Hitchhike over ASAP.
I've got to bury three cigarette butts,

pick my teeth with a foraged dewclaw.
Then I'm free till midnight.

Vigorous exercise is the best cure
for missing someone. And smoking.

Anything that engages the lungs.
Let us compare tails. The tassel

of a lion's contains a spine.
Function: unknown.

Half Hours with Natural History:
Animals Natural and Domestic

*Cross-Departmental Memo, Lion Recreational Department to
Leopard Recreational Department*

WE RAN OUT OF PAPER STOP

PLEASE SEND PAPER AND TOILET PAPER STOP

Please send little battery-operated beetle toys

Please send approval

Please send blimp with air writing capacities so request for approval
can be made via message in
the sky

Please send measurements of female leopard tail STOP

Cross-Departmental Memo, Lion Recreational Department to Leopard Recreational Department

Thank you for collaborating with your colleagues at LRC to achieve departmental goals

Employees request condoms be purchased somewhere other than Dollarama during next order

My brother will not be pursuing any legal action in the recent mauling case

Workplace violence is our number one concern moving into the new fiscal year

We are out of paper again

Cross-Departmental Memo, Lion Recreational Department to
Leopard Recreational Department

Facts about Lions to Ensure Easy Integration into Office
Infrastructure:

The dewclaw on the front limbs is often used as a toothpick

Mother lions, absorbed by some activity, will often forget they have
cubs to care for

Single males, often called nomadic males, live on their own for many
years

It is not unusual for lions to open the abdomen and begin eating while
the animal is still being suffocated

Male cats have spines on their penises that point backwards

The purpose is to cause slight trauma to the female's vagina upon
withdrawal

The pain triggers ovulation

Contrary to popular notion, a lion's eyes do not glow in the dark

Lions fuck like champs in summer and hibernate in cardboard boxes
during winter

If a lion thinks you look like a hot mess, he or she will tell you as much

A lion's capacity for post-coital cuddling is 25 minutes max

Lions struggle to differentiate watching Netflix from looking in the
mirror

Cross-Departmental Memo, Lion Recreational Department to
Leopard Recreational Department

I know you hate when I text you but

I wanted you to know

The butter is so clear in the pan tonight

The rain holding off

The stars almost motile

Medieval Bestiary:
Beast Index

You be the robin. No, you be the crow.
No, the quail. Taxonomically, there's no difference
between a pigeon and a dove, so choose freely.
Doves spend all day making out; pigeons are war

heroes and we still hate them. Be the crocodile:
weep into the swamp post-four-man-meal,
burp up grey beard. Be the withholding swan,
who sings that sweet 'cause she's about to die.

Can't blame sparrows for knocking bluebird
chicks out of the nest, sucking their little bluebird
brains out through their beak-straws.
Can't blame sparrows for all that noise —

they just want to get fucked like everybody else.
I'll be the last-minute beaver, ripping off
my testicles and tossing them in the hunter's path.
My balls being the cure-all for hysteria,

headaches and fever. When another hunter
pursues me, I'll lift my leg so he can see
what he's chasing is already gone.

Evisceration of a Roebuck
with a Portrait of a Married Couple

Cordivologists, ethnobotanists, and physicists gather
here today to study the creaking quantum entanglement of lives:

dead animals and stacked newspapers, instant coffee staining cups —
don't bother to calculate 'cause it's way faster than the speed of light.

The Wu-Tang Clan on windup radios and the murmurations.
The pit stains on white T-shirts and the rings of raven kill.

Recognize my bushy eyebrows as a sign of an unclean mind,
a general attempt at disruptive coloration in western-themed bars.

Tequila shots and sticky quarters widen my perception
of the human-wildlife spatio-temporal interface. Yes, I am guilty

of over-preening to the point of self-injurious behaviour,
but the bald parrot is too easy an analogy. I've never lived

in a cage, and our particles come and go as they please.
Observe closely as I shave the same hair follicle over and over.

Then brush a feather across razor burn. Watch the regrowth
of deer antler, single instance of organ regeneration

in the entire mammalian class. Stem cells and nerves
and blood vessels. Like velvet.

In Defence of My Lawsuit
Against Lubbock Museum

Re: Their Purchase of Two Mules to Be Shot and Stuffed for Exhibit

Should my lawsuit be successful and the animals deemed to require
proper burial, I am fully aware that what will be buried
will no longer be them in their essence, that the parting of meat
and skin was a permanent one formalized on the taxidermist's table.

Are we rendered more or less ourselves by an arrangement of skin?
The difference between hair and fur, between sleekness and drudgery,
between practicality and a dead mule, contained in multitudes of shaved
bone flakes on a hardwood floor.

Personally, I've always felt I was meant to be cotton wrapped
around a wire body, but in this legal transcript I must represent
the best interests of the ghosts of the dead who came to visit me
in line at Subway yesterday morning to insist on justice.

What is justice? I asked them, filling my cup with Fanta
and sitting down with three soft M&M cookies, but they didn't enjoy
talking in such abstract terms, preferring instead to shoot
the shit and split a 12-inch turkey sub, resting their yoke on the table
and blinking away blades of grass that fell lightly from the ceiling.

The Frog-phobic Man

I'm petrified of the little creatures.
— PAUL MARINACCIO SR., PLAINTIFF

What resulted from the flooding of his property was nothing
less than a full-on wetlands, 40 acres of undivided frog horror,
and every Friday night they would use a different mode
of spectacle to torment him, staging eight-hour operas,

rockabilly shows, teenage bush parties, old-fashioned carnivals.
Origins: bullfrogs clutched in a neighbour's hand chasing him
off his childhood property, Old Man Angry and his Bullfrog
Delinquent Enforcers, all parties croaking ancient threats,

a ribbit-ribbit-ing chorus of fuck-yous, supplemented
by a low squeal of workboots. Tame beginnings for a phobia:
no tales of force-fed seared frog legs at tea time, or cowering
in a crumbling well while darting tongues cozied around skinny

ankles. No enlistment to sew his mother's funeral dress
from a thousand slimy bellies. Brain cells trigger brain cells
triggering a heart to pound at the sight of amphibian gangs,
a blooming cold sore on a bank teller's face, invisible

salmonella deathrays beamed from freshly shredded lettuce.
If you're going to put a price on it, I'd say $1.3 million,
$328,400 for compensatory damages, $250,000 in punitive
damages, plus help that man dig ditches to dry out the land,

keep digging until we strike it rich when our shovels touch
what is rational, mud reverting to hard dirt, hearts
beating in time to the grinding of our teeth.
"I'm going to put cows out there," Marinaccio said.

Project Isabela

The ultimate goal of Project Isabela, initiated in 1997 and completed in 2006, was the eventual restoration of Pinta and Santiago Islands and the larger, northern portion of Isabela Island. The project began in response to the massive destruction by introduced goats of both native vegetation and terrain. The goat population on northern Isabela was estimated at 100,000 animals.

— GALAPAGOS CONSERVANCY

PLEASE SELECT PLAYERS:

Level 1, Player 1

How will it be when you can choose
what you turn into — let me rephrase:
what kind of creature are you?

Level 1, Player 2

I birth myself as prehistoric
pterodactyl hellhound — call me
the eternal wolfening 'cause
I'm about to tear into this isle
of pussies with sorrowful
teeth and a mathematical mind.

Level 2, Player 1

The Judas goat isn't trying to mislead you
with her permanent ovulation. Come closer.
Who each of us would follow anywhere
is a personal question, bound by helixes of sex,

geography and mobility. I've played
this once before, right? a) in another lifetime,
b) on my Game Boy, c) surrounded by palm trees.

Level 2, Player 2

Aerial sharpshooters and super
Judas goat subterfuge: twin lures
of Galapagos ferality reduction.
An unexpected war zone in paradise,
German shepherds all up in the archipelagos,
50 goats per hour, 500,000 rounds
of ammo. I kill-shot the billy goat;
tortoises transmit appreciation
via gold coins and fresh
water drained from bladders.

Level 3, Player 1

When you feel yourself herded by an invisible hand,
check for radio tags and chemical injections
sending coded messages to your genitals.
Advance. Retreat. Grow kill count.
Easy tip for hungry colonialist sailors:
stack tortoises shell-down for an easy,
nutrient-packed snack that stays alive
for 365 days with zero food or water.

Level 3, Player 2

I rack up 9000 points — as anticipated,
the tortoises form stepping stones
for my blistered feet.
The tortoises' eyes spill red
hearts into blue ocean,
spawning smaller pink hearts.

Level 3, Player 1, Part II

Everything not saved will be lost.
You have travelled very far and overcome many obstacles.
Measure your wonder / open your toolkit.
This cordate leaf is heart-shaped.
This sagittate leaf is arrow-shaped.
A reniform leaf is kidney-shaped.
Cordivology is the study of crows
learning to chronologize their own feathers.

I.

II.

III.

Dead Mule Zone IV:
Overwork

Supervisor:

You're not paid overtime unless you work 44+ hours,
so if you've put in 43 hours, it's to your financial
benefit to stay another 1.5. Anything you contribute
to the company blog will be on your own time.

Mule:

So difficult to choose my favourite animal YouTube video,
but I'd have to go with the owl petting dog.

Supervisor:

Your type of appendages, specifically shiny black hooves,
are unlikely to develop carpal tunnel syndrome, but if you do,
your benefits kick in after three months of full-time employment.

Mule:

As if we too might be hanging out by the backdoor sprinkler
and find new and miraculous uses for our claws,
and, if we're being cynical, and the owl was just picking nits
out of the dog's hair, that an audience of four million
might mistakenly view our killer appendages as tender,
that a single 2:44 clip might erase a vivid history
of soft white mice ripped to shreds.

Supervisor:

The upper left corner of the Pizza Pizza sign will always
be visible from your desk. It doesn't undulate in the wind,
change colour at sunset or fall to pieces and rebuild itself
every hour. That's just your imagination.

Mule:

Do I relate to the owl or the dog?
It depends. A hoof is to a claw is to a hand
is to a paw. Sometimes pizza grease smears itself
across the skyline in primitive smoked-pink messages.
Sometimes a red crane moves across the ceiling-to-floor
glass window and the man inside waves at you
and part of you moves with it.

So I guess I would like to know if it's fundamentally
a question about freedom. Before I answer the question.

Extirpation

Geography never repeats itself.
The Tasmanian tiger live-tweets its extinction
from the Hobart zoo in 1933;
aurochs fling feces with their Holocene horns
across centuries, get dirty looks from HR.
Popular opinion shifts ever-so-seismically.
Good pets with bad press are still fucked;
terms of venery mean the world to me.
Everyone stops calling — epochs beget epochs
between Friday night plans.
I murder your white hens, eviscerate
shell and feather indiscriminately,
smear blood all over your white chicken coop.
My eyes are beady. I ate your Greek yoghurt
from the communal fridge.
I net only four percent of the Who Wore It Better vote,
the wolves having accessorized the blood
more elegantly by dragging their snouts
across fresh snow. I heard it
from the school of cod I used to hang with,
saw rumour vibrate from shell to shell
among the zebra mussels.
I've only ever eaten my share and then some.
Similar to the last known passenger pigeon,
I was last sighted in a flock of regular pigeons,
fitting right in.

If I Were a Killer Whale

When my supervisor asked me to stay 10 minutes late
to edit a press release for First Quantum Minerals,
I'd fuckin' rip off his arm while wearing a super
elegant black and white tuxedo jacket.

You *should* be scared. But let us not draw parallels
between captivities with our dry-erase markers too closely.
Instead collage photos of zebra carcasses, trim them
in snake skin, present them to ourselves as evidence

we still have a taste for the really fishy fish despite
our demure eye makeup. I don't need to be reminded
I'm human — I have four plastic containers of pythons
beneath my desk, a tin of sardines under my keyboard,

and leather underwear. I don't eat meat, but I love to wear it
and wrap it around blue cheese for shark fishing at dawn.
Like the killer whale, I don't want to eat your arm.
I just want to take it away from you.

Re: My wardrobe this week. My hair's in a bun
and I picked up a T-shirt in Chinatown with three wolves
howling at a puffy moon to wear to the meeting.
So you'll see me coming.

Dead Mule Zone V: Old Age

Supervisor:

You are sitting at your desk. Pretend 22 years have passed —
or better yet, wait for 22 years to pass.

[Pause for 22 years]

You are sitting at your desk.

Mule:

What made me stay? So many gorillas weeping
over fluffy handfuls of dead kittens, so many newborn
white tiger triplets suckling golden retriever nipples,
so much playful interspecies swatting. Raccoons
stealing carpets. Blind poodles rescued from garbage heaps.

Supervisor:

Owl Love for Dog,
Tiger and Dog Are Best Friends,
Fox Kit Becomes Friends with Dog,
Cheetah and Dog Friends Celebrate:
well-documented favourites of yours.

Mule:

It's true YouTube ruined my life, rationing just enough
shaky wild animal footage to continue, though sometimes,
as you know, I would spill coffee across my desk on purpose.

It's true I won departmental MVP twice in three years,
and I do consider it a great accomplishment.

It's true I have nearly uncontrollable urges to trample
soft ducklings in woodsheds, but grind my teeth instead.

Supervisor:

It's true I never convinced you of the insurmountable proof
I obtained from extensive research and data analysis,
despite my numerous graphs and flow charts — namely,
that the owl and the dog never loved one other.
It's true you never heard the gorillas weeping.
Your computer volume has been muted for 21 years.

It's true I always found the wet black eyes of animals
cloying and off-putting, as shocking as the yellow leaves
and cicada shells that accumulate around your desk
until the janitor vacuums on Fridays,
though I've never mentioned it until now.

Maybe the baby falcon should have a timeout.
Please punish it, because I'm afraid I'll never
love anything as much. For example,
the smell of vanilla can mask reductions
in sugar up to 25 percent. Me & you &
the ol' spinach in the brownies trick.
That beak. How to make infant talons less
palatable to the refined unemployed adult
taste bud. Yes, but the wings are my favourite
part of the bird because they taste good
and are aspirational. I should put on my
Fly Like a Falcon workout DVD because
I'm feeling revved by its tufted BMI.
The only way to be healthy without you —
engineer a low fat Snickers bar from kale,
yellow beets and errant hairs in the drain.
Or become an avid member of the Canadian
Peregrine Foundation. Membership pending.
I'm on the zero calorie wistful binocular diet.
I'm having an obesogenic field day in the low
fat caramel avian tasting lab today. My life
is feathers and aspartame. I quit my job
to spend more time researching eagles.
I said eagles but I meant falcons. They're not
ever coming back. I like the way they look
but I hate how smart they are. You know?

Evidence for Rational Thought in Animals

What I do in my dreams in my own business,
but if you must know, I cause horrible bus accidents.
No, I don't drive in the sense that I'm not licensed
and don't know how to do it.
I just get so wound up sometimes.
Bike cops chase me round the roundabouts,
crash into hot dog stands. I scoop up
the corn relish, let the sidewalk's natural vinegars
pickle the onions. I will find you always,
my hound, as you circle back again and again
to scented cement, not knowing
the direction your own tail is pointing.
How do you go about acquiring a big vocabulary?
I want to prepare for my flashback 10 years ago
where I run over an English bulldog in my red van
and emote. Guttural whimpering doesn't fool me.
I must be able to adequately represent
my internal debate about an animal's capacity
for rational thought during the impending
manslaughter trial. Exhibit A: paw bent
unnaturally towards a horizon, ears pinned back
in accusatory recognition. Exhibit B:
There's that horse that can do math.
That means something, like how the more
my muscles tighten, the more I feel capable of violence.
You'll never be alone because bloodshot eyes
excite me too. I'm not on my side, but the jury
hung itself on the central fact that, buddy,
drooling makes you look dumb.

Dead Mule Zone VI:
Submersion in Domestic Metaphor

Domestic Partner:

Cashew nut chicken,	
stir fried chicken & veggies w/ brown sauce	8.50?
Basil chicken (beef),	
stir fried chicken & veggies w/ basil sauce	8.50?
Canadian broccoli,	
stir fried with garlic sauce	6.95?
Sesame chicken,	
battered, wok 'em w/ Szechuan sauce	7.95?

Mule:

At first I didn't realize the girl was weeping on the subway.
There was a man holding a plastic bag full of yellow tulips,
and a woman in a leopard print beret and neon heels.
I looked at an ad for massage therapy college courses for a while
and got kind of turned on and missed my stop completely.

Domestic Partner:

I know you say the amount of mud you track into the apartment
is beyond your control, but sometimes it seems like you smear it
all over the door handles on purpose.

Mule:

Do you think she would have stopped crying if the man had given
her the bag of tulips? Do you think the woman looked okay in that hat?
I would say a) there's nothing sadder than flowers in a plastic bag, so no;
and b) yes — although several hairs sprouted out of her left ear,

the woman arranged a fan of bobby pins that was so hypnotizing,
I missed my stop completely.

Domestic Partner:

Have you seen the Tupperware with the blue lid so we can eat
this for lunch tomorrow? Was there a subway delay this morning?
Why is there a bottle of Canadian Club in the bathroom?

Mule:

It's hard to say — I thought my dog was pretty much human,
and then I caught him eating vomit in the park, face burrowed
in leaves beside a picnic table, slurping in the sun.

Self-Evaluation for Employee #M100656984

Please check all skills that apply and expand in the box provided below.

☐ MULTI-TASKING — *Please provide recent example.*

Last night I mainlined 14 orange Pixy Stix while reading the entire May 2010 issue of *InStyle* magazine.

This afternoon, my nose bled while I ate a bruised peach and streamed videos of coyotes howling at the moon on my double screen monitor (no sound).

☐ ATTENTION TO DETAIL — *Please provide recent example.*

On Tuesday I started googling uncircumcised penises and couldn't stop. Then I investigated vaginal prolapses and ended up staying overtime. I was determined to render lifelike drawings by end of market close and succeeded in my goal.

The white on the far left walls is different than the white on the far right walls. One is the uneasy sunny side up jiggle of egg under environmentally friendly LED lights. The other is a blister reflected in a tin can.

☐ TEAM WORK — *Please provide recent example.*

I had a sex dream of a threesome with the Romanian woman in IT and the CTO with an abundance of nose hair. They were both competent in their fields.

☐ INNOVATION — *Please provide recent example.*

I feel the mouse I caught in my kitchen and subsequently released in the staff bathrooms will contribute a value-added role to our company. Everyone loves a cuddly little grey triangle, and I am confident he will earn mascot-like levels of affection in the coming weeks.

Chewing on staples makes my gums bleed, but it increases my alertness and ability to distinguish living and inanimate shapes from one another.

The Neighbour

You're balled up in the farthest left corner of the deck,
too lazy or rabid to move on.

Alternately yawning and looking alarmed,
accepting bread, dragging your tail in the ashtray.

Do you want me to describe your features?
The mask? The eyelashes? Those dexterous paws?

I've seen you here before, and you get prettier with age,
just like me. Do you love what you do?

I wasn't born to live like you, but maybe I could.
That piece of bread is for you. You can have

the cigarette butts too. I was born to watch prime time
teen shows in the morning, to eat granola bars on the toilet

while reading two different fashion magazines at once.
To build a monument of plaid shirts on a bedroom floor,

to watch dust rise and settle on necklace chains.
You're moving on now, packing up for the day.

I toss the silver granola bar wrapper at you,
but you've already hit the pavement.

I assumed because you eat from the garbage,
you'll eat anything. Kind of like thinking my freckles

don't know one other. Or assuming bedbugs would want
to live in my apartment at all.

23rd Session between Mule and Psychiatrist

2013-05-05

So you've been feeling anxious again?

I can't sleep at night. I imagine my body as an itchy dandelion stem and I spend the night lying in bed scratching with a boar-bristle hairbrush.

Are you still worried your parents will die if you don't recite a Wallace Stevens poem backwards and forwards every night before you go to bed?

I solved that problem by printing all his poems on a sheet of bristol board in the shape of an okapi and gluing it to my ceiling, which is the opposite of what you told me to do. My main worry is the lobster I ate for dinner on Friday night.

You feel guilty about eating the lobster for ethical reasons, or are you troubled by the extravagance of the meal?

I don't usually eat lobster but my boss was paying. I'm concerned about it reassembling itself inside my stomach, claw by hepatopancreas by thorax by eye.

Well you didn't eat the whole lobster with the shell and eyes and everything anyway, did you?

Yeah, I did.

What is your concern about the lobster rebuilding itself inside you? That it will torment you and rip up your insides?

I don't think he would do that to me. All I've heard so far is a faint click / clack of claws when I lie on my back at night and look at my map of Canada from 1812. A knowledge of bulging eyes inside me. Antennae pointing north.

What are you afraid of then?

That he'll divide me. That there will be one me, with a full-time job and domestic partner and hobbies like cooking, photography and printmaking, and another me, a reassembled lobster-ghost who lies on his back in a bowel stew, looking up at the stars.

So a shadow self in the form of a dead lobster you ate for dinner once?

Yes. The breeze in my stomach is cold in the spring.

Did I hear you describe yourself as human?

No, I don't think so.

Dead Mule Zone VII:
Fall into Subterranean Cavity

Supervisor:

It's a shame you only lasted one year and five months,
but we wish you all the best in your new position,
which appears a custom fit to your unique work style
and aptitude for manual labour.

Your dishevelled, animalistic aesthetic combined
with your propensity for emotional displays and clear
favouritism for working class values, not to mention
your obsessive email forwards of cute animal pics

on BuzzFeed and awkward last ditch attempts
at professionalism towards the end of each month,
made you an interesting but challenging
colleague in a high-volume, team-oriented environment.

Mule:

Strange how the plough feels right and not right at the same time,
until the second the earth caves in, and I am happy to report
that such subterranean cavities are exactly as you imagine,
with upside down greying fields of corn and apple orchards

of windy red, littered with skeletons of long-dead farm dogs,
eternally pregnant cats with rabies-twisted bodies,
and fluorescent worms that long to be cupped in your hands.

For the record, the plough died the most painful death,
all those yellow machine parts falling away from each other
as they tried to catch one last glimpse of the shiny barn
and parallel ruts left behind.

Supervisor:

When I picture you falling, it lasts two minutes
and 14 seconds, and though I know three of your legs
broke upon impact, I envision you pulling the plough
1.2 more miles underground before the dirt fills

your ears. The music in the background is different
each time, and depending on the day of week
and general workload around the office,
I pause it a split second before the end and play it over again.

Instant Messaging Session
Between Two Employees at Mule's Work

May 22, 2013

what was the cause of death?

watching too many sloth YouTube videos at work

? is that a metaphor?

ha no

thats not a cause of death

his liver turned puke-silver and grease from all the burritos and chocolate chips from all the breakfast MMMuffins and the miniscule pieces of glass he had been ingesting secretly at break over the course of 9 years seeped out

the fire alarm went off but the voice on the intercom said they were only evacuating floors 1 to 8

i doubt it was a sloth video, it was probably the one where the honey badger bites the cobra's head off

at first I thought it was the one where the sloth is sitting in a high chair like some ridiculous prehistoric dog child and it presents the volunteer with a red flower

that flower is totally just stuck to his claw

i refuse to believe that

so which video?

forensics still has to confirm, but they believe it's the one of the sloth swimming beside the boat. the sloth looks like a majestic wet blanket coasting along the water, surprisingly adept at this motion, like he finally realized he could defeat the slowness that has plagued him all his life

maybe he was never plagued by slowness. maybe he liked being slow

yeah maybe

so he had never seen a sloth swim before. he didn't know a sloth could swim like that. and it changed everything.

yep

man I actually don't really even know how to use excel

?

oh haha sorry I was talking to someone else

Decoherence
After *Young Horses* by Emil Nolde

The poem presupposes a natural lifespan,
two young horses,
quantum-entangled against German landscape,
ungalata-d neck-to-neck
like two violins trying to break each other apart.

You broke a sweat lately?
You ever broke a sweat in your life?

When I was a young horse,
I effervesced all over myself, aerodynamic
and crepuscular, muted and oily.
The poem presupposes symmetry and a desire to live
a good life, a good life like the life
a young horse has.

When I was a young horse,
I put bells on everything,
and all the young horses
were repainted the colour of robins.

You want to get ripped?
You want to blow off steam and streamline your body?
The poem presupposes
that's a great life for some people.

When I was a young horse,
I built secret quantum computers
in mugs of cold coffee,
learned to gently deep throat weather
vanes on country estates.

You want big muscles and delicate ears?
You want a body nobody finds repulsive?
When I was a young horse,
I wanted it.

When I was a young horse,
I would walk
down the street singing abattoir blues,
and people would remind me I wasn't that young.

Supervisor's Memo:
The Starburst Has Been Sitting There
Since 1989

Though I have a fondness for birdwatching and garbage picking,
I have never cared much about the way other people live,

the destruction of the mythic American road trip and construction
of Toronto–Montreal super highways being no great loss to me.

I'd rather see the comforting steel of smokestacks as I drive by
at 120 KMPH, pyramids of twisted scrap metal pointing haphazardly

to the stars, the sharp silver outline of 10,000 cars compressed
into 12 x 12 metres. The ability to transform something large

into something tiny is a quality I have always admired
in human or machine. I grew up in a small town,

and the thought of the ceramic dog sculptures lining the shelves
of the convenience store and its discreet adult movies room,

the fingerprint-smeared bins of stale Swedish Berries, makes me
long for the comfort of a slick Christmas-neon 7-Eleven sign.

Sometimes you look up from shoplifting Hot Rods and the cashier
is watching you in the freezer door glass, pity superimposed

on 2% milk. The Russian wolfhound is 50% off, the Skittles are two
for one, and there's a fine coating of dust on everything.

Sometimes you want to sit at your desk and eat rock
hard candy until your teeth give in.

Ruminations by Mule
in Mule & Cowboy Painting
on Your Parents' Living Room Wall

Kindness is slanted here. The stream is melted Dr Pepper
Slurpees with 7-Eleven hot dog drippings flashing like greasy eels.

They slip between his fingers as he tries to drink, and this,
combined with half a scrawled sun glimpsed in the corner

of an eye for eternity, turns us both mean and desert-faced.
Nobody bothered to draw the sun well and now we're stuck

with it. A sun learns to see itself as ugly through daily lessons
and an undisputable mathematical formula written in red Freezies.

Your mom thinks he's squinting due to his stoicism and historical
cowboy nature. Really, he's just exhausted by his thirst and the sun's

ugliness. We went to school to learn to be kind to one another,
but it didn't last. He knew on which notch I preferred my saddle,

but didn't always choose it. He suffered from arthritis, nostalgia
and an intense desire to eat dirt when it grew hot in the afternoon.

I licked rocks and humped rope. I found it difficult to live
in a 2 x 3 foot space, so much of it impressionistic shrubbery.

No sharp lines meant nowhere to hang myself on the crayon horizon.
I lied. The water tastes like water. It's water despite the glucose-

fructose undertones and heavy-handed western shadows.
When he lifts his hands to his mouth to drink, the cowboy hat

slides forward and vibrates with its own music. It's playing
a blade of grass in the future, in the next scene, one town over.

Notes

The "Dead Mule Zone" poems are inspired by Jerry Leath Mills's essay on (you guessed it) dead mules in Southern literature entitled "The Dead Mule Rides Again." All titles are named after the various methods of demise outlined by Mills in his argument.

"Messianic Age" is dedicated to the deer that wandered into the downtown Toronto core on November 24, 2009.

"Past & Future Lives with My Best Friend, Who Is Mushrooms" is loosely based on Hamilton Morris's investigative piece on psilocybin mushrooms and murder entitled "Blood Spore" in *Harper's Magazine*.

The facts presented in "Did You Know? Fun Facts About Mules" are from the Canadian Donkey and Mule Association's website, though they don't claim these facts are fun at any point.

The quotation at the beginning of "Materials for a Memoir on Animal Locomotion" is an actual thing George Adamson said about his wife, Joy Adamson.

Some of the facts about lions in "Half Hours with Natural History: Animals Natural and Domestic" are from the aptly named website Lion Facts.

Acknowledgements

Earlier versions of some poems appeared in print or online in the pages of *Riddle Fence*, *The Puritan*, *Grain* and *The Collagist*, as well as on iTunes via the Writers' Trust of Canada (which reminds me, thanks to the Writers' Trust for their support, enthusiasm and all the good work they do).

I am grateful for the support of the Toronto Arts Council, the Ontario Arts Council and the Canada Council during the completion of this project. Many thanks to the Banff Centre for my time at the writing studio, and to Karen Solie and Suzanne Buffam for their mentorship.

Thank you to my ever-rotating poetry workshop for their encouragement and input, especially mainstays Phoebe Wang, Catriona Wright, Ted Nolan, Bardia Sinaee & Matt Loney. Thanks to Suzannah Showler for introducing me to ECW Press.

Thanks to all the amazing folks at ECW, especially Michael Holmes for the edit, Emily Schultz for the copyedit, and Natalie Olsen for the dead-on cover design.

Thanks always to my supportive & book-loving family.

Published by ECW Press
665 Gerrard Street East, Toronto, Ontario, Canada M4M 1Y2
416-694-3348 / info@ecwpress.com

Get the eBook Free
Purchase the print edition and receive the eBook free!
For details, go to ecwpress.com/eBook.

Library and Archives Canada Cataloguing in Publication

Clarke, Laura, 1985-, author
Decline of the animal kingdom /
Laura Clarke.

Poems.

Issued in print and electronic formats.
ISBN 978-1-77041-282-8 (pbk.)
ISBN 978-1-77090-802-4 (pdf)
ISBN 978-1-77090-803-1 (epub)

I. Title.

PS8605.L36645D42 2015   C811'.6   C2015-902780-2
C2015-902781-0

Editor for the press: Michael Holmes | a misFit book
Cover design: Natalie Olsen | kisscut design
Cover image: Jonas Bros. of Denver Taxidermy Catalogue, circa 1967
Interior images: from Christian Heinrich Pander's *Die vergleichende Osteologie* (1821)
Author photo: Phoebe Wang
Type: Rachel Ironstone

MISFIT

Coach House Printing   5   4   3   2   1

The publication of *Decline of the Animal Kingdom* has been generously supported by the Canada Council for the Arts which last year invested $153 million to bring the arts to Canadians throughout the country, and by the Government of Canada through the Canada Book Fund. *Nous remercions le Conseil des arts du Canada de son soutien. L'an dernier, le Conseil a investi 153 millions de dollars pour mettre de l'art dans la vie des Canadiennes et des Canadiens de tout le pays. Ce livre est financé en partie par le gouvernement du Canada.* We also acknowledge the Ontario Arts Council (OAC), an agency of the Government of Ontario, which last year funded 1,709 individual artists and 1,078 organizations in 204 communities across Ontario, for a total of $52.1 million, and the contribution of the Government of Ontario through the Ontario Book Publishing Tax Credit and the Ontario Media Development Corporation.

Canada Council
for the Arts

Conseil des Arts
du Canada

Canada

Ontario

Ontario Media Development
Corporation

ONTARIO ARTS COUNCIL
CONSEIL DES ARTS DE L'ONTARIO

an Ontario government agency
un organisme du gouvernement de l'Ontario

Printed and bound in Canada